Britain in the Past
The Iron Age

Moira Butterfield

W

FRANKLIN WATTS

LONDON · SYDNEY

Franklin Watts
First published in 2015 by the Watts Publishing Group

Editor: Sarah Ridley
Editor in chief: John C. Miles
Series designer: Jane Hawkins
Art director: Peter Scoulding
Picture research: Diana Morris

Picture credits:
AA World Travel Library/Alamy: 4c. © Ashmolean Museum. University of Oxford: 24b.
British Museum, London: 25. British Museum, London. Gift of J S Rymer: 17l, 17r. British Museum/
Munoz-Yague/SPL: 13t, 13b. Chiociolla/Shutterstock: 11b. Eastern Daily Press: 22b. Greg Balfour
Evans/Alamy: 29. Foaloce/Dreamstime: 21t. Werner Forman Archive/Alamy: 1, 4tl, 6tl, 8tl, 10tl,
12tl, 14tl, 16tl, 18tl, 19, 20tl, 22tl, 24tl, 26tl, 28tl. Gabriel12/5/Shutterstock: 12b. Andriy Gusak/
Shutterstock: 5. © Hampshire County Council/courtesy of the Hampshire Cultural Trust: 14b. In the
Museum of the Iron Age, Andover: 14b. Helen Hotson/Shutterstock: 21b. Last Refuge/Robert Harding
PL: 6c. Dieter Lion/Dreamstime: 9. David Lyons/age fotostock/Superstock: 8b. Andrew McLean/
Shutterstock: 10b. Stephan Mulcahey/Alamy: 26c. National Museum Wales: 11t, 20c. © Oxford
University & The Portable Antiquities Scheme: 7. CC. PAS: 16b. Radharc Images/Alamy: 15. Skyscan
Photolibrary/Alamy: front cover. Thomasamm/Dreamstime: 18c. Fabrizio Troiani/Dreamstime: 27.
Nick Turner/Alamy: 28b. Steve Vidler/Alamy: 23.

Dewey number: 941

Hardback ISBN: 978 1 4451 4063 6
Library eBook ISBN: 978 1 4451 4064 3

Printed in China

Franklin Watts
An imprint of
Hachette Children's Group
Part of The Watts Publishing Group
Carmelite House
50 Victoria Embankment
London EC4Y 0DZ

An Hachette UK Company
www.hachette.co.uk
www.franklinwatts.co.uk

Contents

Enter the Iron Age

We split British history into periods of time with different names. We call the time between 800 BCE and 43 CE the Iron Age. It was roughly between 2,000 and 3,000 years ago.

▲ At the beginning of the Iron Age people lived in small villages like this one, reconstructed in Hampshire.

Iron arrives

The very first people in Britain used stone tools, in a time we call the Stone Age. After that came a time called the Bronze Age, when tools and weapons were made of bronze. Then, around 3,000 years ago, the secrets of making iron arrived in Britain from Europe. Iron was cheaper and much tougher than bronze. Iron axes, plough parts and sickles (for cutting

If you lived in the Iron Age...

At the beginning of the Iron Age you would not have known many people. There were probably less than a million people in the whole of the country (now there are around 64 million).

crops) soon became popular because they made farming easier.

Iron Age beginnings

At the beginning of the Iron Age people lived in small villages and spent their days growing crops and looking after farm animals. Their homes were roundhouses, with a thatched roof shaped like a witch's hat. The walls were made from woven branches plastered with mud, and everybody lived in one big dark room inside.

Making iron

To make iron, Iron Age people first had to collect iron ore, rocks that contain iron and can be found near the surface of the ground. The iron ore had to be heated in clay furnaces, then beaten, heated and beaten over and over again to make strong iron metal that could be shaped in different ways.

Magical iron

Iron Age blacksmiths must have been very important people. Only they knew the secrets of making iron, and people might even have thought they had magical powers.

Climb to a hill fort

Better farming meant more food for everyone. Soon the number of people in Britain rose, and tribes grew, too. A tribe is a group of people who live in one area, with their own leaders.

Maiden Castle, a big Iron Age hill fort in Dorset. ▼

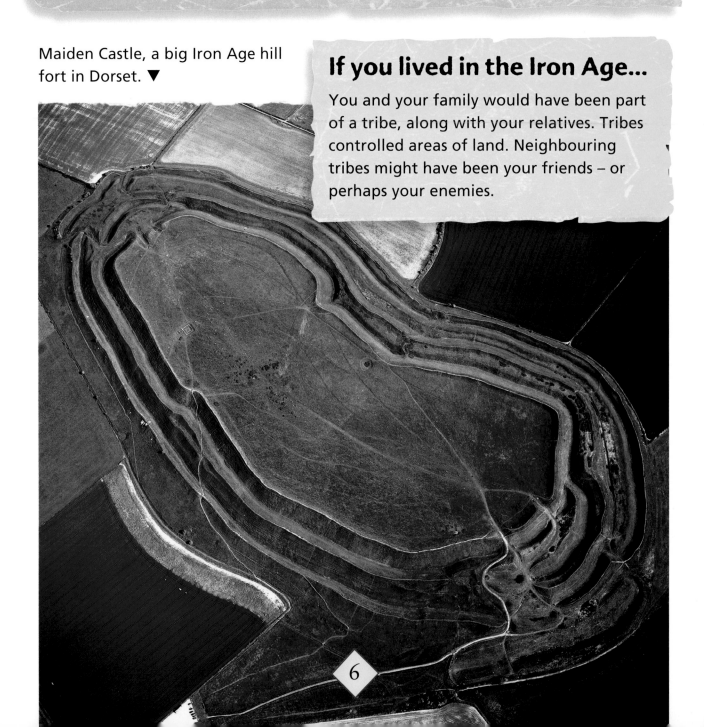

If you lived in the Iron Age...

You and your family would have been part of a tribe, along with your relatives. Tribes controlled areas of land. Neighbouring tribes might have been your friends – or perhaps your enemies.

Here we are!

Tribes used hill forts as bases. They were built on top of high hills, where there was a good view and the forts could be seen for miles around. They sent out the message to anyone who saw them: *"This is our land!"*. One of the biggest hill forts in the whole of Europe was at Maiden Castle in Dorset. It once covered an area the size of 50 football pitches! Its name comes from 'Mai Du', Iron Age words for 'great hill'.

Inside a hill fort

Inside Maiden Castle there was room for several hundred people living in lots of roundhouses. There were food stores and workshops, too. The fort was surrounded by deep ditches and high earth banks. These were topped with a fence of wooden stakes called a palisade, making it hard for attackers to get inside.

Who lived here?

The Durotriges (*dure-oh-tree-gaze*) tribe lived at Maiden Castle. They left behind all sorts

Look!

In the late Iron Age the Durotriges tribe made their own coins (shown here), some of which have been found at Maiden Castle. There is no writing on the coins, so we don't know the names of their leaders.

◀ Coins made by the Durotriges tribe, who lived at Maiden Castle. ▼

of everyday objects such as pieces of pottery and equipment for weaving and metal-making. Archaeologists discovered an Iron Age cemetery where people were buried with belongings such as jewellery and even food. Perhaps their families believed they would need them in an afterlife. Some of the skeletons were warriors who had been killed in battle.

Sleep in a broch

By the middle of the Iron Age there were clear differences in the way people lived in different parts of Britain. While people in the south were building hill forts, people in the far north were building sturdy stone towers called brochs.

Enemies approaching!

Over 500 brochs have been found in northern Scotland, mainly on the coast. Each broch had hollow walls with a winding staircase inside, leading up to the top of the tower. They made good enemy lookout towers, and it's possible people hid inside them when there was trouble. The best preserved tower is the Broch of Gurness on Orkney, (below)

Look!

The broch builders had no concrete. They built the tower by hand, piling up stones to make it wide at the bottom and narrower in the middle. It was incredibly skilful building, and nobody in modern times has been able to copy it successfully!

▲ The entrance of the broch (above) could be blocked shut from the inside.

If you lived in the Iron Age...

You would have been kept busy from an early age, helping with farm animals and learning skills such as grinding wheat with a stone to make bread flour.
A big grinding stone, called a quern, was found in one of the Gurness houses.

others may have come to hide when necessary. The tower was around 8 m high and once had a massive wooden door and timbers to bar it shut on the inside in times of trouble.

Tower of power

The broch had a living room with smaller rooms around the outside, and rooms upstairs as well as downstairs. It had its own freshwater well inside, as well as a hearth, cupboards, beds and a toilet all made from stone. Perhaps the most important family in the local tribe lived here, but we don't know for sure.

which has the remains of Iron Age stone houses around it.

Sitting on stone

The houses around the Broch of Gurness were built inside a high earth bank and a ditch to stop attacks. Up to 40 families could have lived here, and perhaps

Eat at a feast

People got together to feast in Iron Age times. We know this from food and pottery remains found at places where they gathered.

Feasting on water

At Loch Tay in Scotland divers have found the remains of nearly 20 crannogs – large roundhouses that were built on platforms sticking out into the water. One of the crannogs has been reconstructed (below).

A reconstructed crannog roundhouse on Loch Tay. ▼

Look!

Metal pieces called firedogs held up the meat spit on either side of an Iron Age fire. This firedog, found at Capel Garmon in North Wales, was finely made and probably designed to impress guests!

roasted over a fire. The divers even found wooden plates, some preserved sloes that had been picked ready to eat and a butter dish with some butter still in it!

Festival time

At East Chisenbury in Wiltshire archaeologists have found a huge feasting site from the early Iron Age. Pottery and animal bones from the feasting lie thickly on the ground over a wide area. It seems that Iron Age crowds once came here, along with herds of animals, for a big festival. Perhaps different tribes met up here every year.

As well as house remains, the cold peaty waters of the loch have preserved the food remains from fine Iron Age feasts. Perhaps tribal leaders held feasts for their people here.

Wild menu

The people who lived at Loch Tay foraged (looked) for edible wild plants and mushrooms to eat. More than 160 different types of edible plant remains have been found in the loch, as well as bones from wild animals and farm animals that were

If you lived in the Iron Age...

You would be used to eating wild plants such as chickweed and sorrel (below), which has a lemony taste. You would use wild plants to make medicine, too.

Discover a murder

Grisly evidence of Iron Age human sacrifices have been rediscovered in locations around northern Europe, including Britain.

Peat bog bodies

The bodies of murdered Iron Age men and women have turned up in places which were once marshy peat bogs or lakes. We know that Iron Age people sometimes threw valuable possessions into water, perhaps as offerings to their gods and goddesses, and it's possible they sometimes sacrificed people for the same reason.

Sacrifice to a god

In 1984 workmen discovered Lindow Man in an ancient peat bog in Cheshire. He had been murdered in the late Iron Age and pushed into the water face

Look!

This picture shows a peat bog in Northern Ireland. Peat is a kind of crumbly soil made from plants that have rotted over thousands of years. It contains chemicals that have helped to preserve Iron Age bodies, even the skin and hair.

down. Chemicals in the peat had preserved his body, including his skin and hair. Scientists have even been able to work out that before Lindow Man died he ate bread cooked over a fire and the pollen of mistletoe, a plant that late Iron Age people believed was magical. Perhaps his final meal was part of a religious ceremony.

Moustache man

Experts have been able to reconstruct the face of Lindow Man. He had dark hair and a neatly-trimmed beard and moustache (moustaches were a popular fashion in Iron Age times).

▲ A hologram of Lindow Man's head and shoulders.

A reconstruction of Lindow Man's head and shoulders. ▼

If you lived in the Iron Age...

You would have believed in gods and goddesses that controlled the world and were to be found in natural places such as lakes and woods.

Ride with warriors

By the middle of the Iron Age we know that there was regular fighting between tribes. The men in a tribe would have had to learn how to fight, using iron swords and iron-tipped spears.

A story in bones

At Danebury, a big Iron Age hill fort in Hampshire, archaeologists uncovered a pit full of human bones that were marked with battle injuries made by Iron Age weapons such as spears. Three other hill forts can be seen from Danebury, and it's possible that battles were fought with these other nearby tribes. Perhaps these near neighbours were fighting for control of the local land.

Look!

Skulls found at Danebury, such as the one below, had holes in them made by Iron Age spears.

Iron Age spearhead of the type used to kill people at Danebury. ▼

On horseback

At Danebury a buried horse was found with marks on its skeleton and teeth that prove that it had been ridden by a human and had worn a bit in its mouth. This is the first example of any horse being ridden in Britain. We know that in the late Iron Age warriors went into battle on horse-drawn chariots. Perhaps the Danebury warriors were amongst the first to ride into war.

Blue in battle

Around 5,000 years ago an ancient Greek explorer called Pytheas visited Iron Age Britain and wrote about what he found. He called the people the 'Pretani', meaning 'painted people', and we know that Iron Age British warriors painted their bodies blue and perhaps even tattooed themselves. They used natural plants and berries to create the blue colour.

This re-enactor is carrying a spear similar to those used in Iron Age battles. ▶

If you lived in the Iron Age...

Warriors would probably have become the tribal leaders in Iron Age times. Everybody would have admired and obeyed them.

15

Meet two VIPs

Iron Age burials are rare to find, but some of the grandest examples have been discovered in East Yorkshire. Here local leaders were buried along with possessions and food, probably for them to take on a journey to an afterlife.

Magical mirror?

Around 300 BCE a woman was buried at Wetwang in Yorkshire along with the wheels and frame of a chariot, some food and an engraved metal shape rather like a mirror. When it was polished it would only have shown a very blurred reflection, though, so some people have suggested that the lady might have used the

If you lived in the Iron Age...

If you were an ordinary person you wouldn't have been able to afford fine swords or mirrors. These things would have belonged to the wealthy leaders of your tribe.

▲ The mirror found at Wetwang was very worn and damaged, but would once have been similar to this one, which was found at Shillington, Bedfordshire.

object in a ceremony. Perhaps she thought the reflection showed her a magical world of gods and goddesses.

Sign of the spears

In nearby Kirkburn in Yorkshire an important warrior was buried with one of the finest Iron Age swords ever found, called the Kirkburn Sword. Once the warrior's grave was filled in, three iron spears were stuck down into it from above. There they stayed for many years marking his grave, perhaps so that everybody would remember his battle bravery.

The Kirkburn Sword belonged to a man in his late 20s or early 30s – an old man in Iron Age society. ▶

▲ Can you see the decoration on the top of the sword? It would have been expensive to make.

Look!

The Kirkburn Sword was skilfully made and decorated with bronze, red glass and animal horn. Its wealthy owner once had it repaired, perhaps after a battle.

Make some art

The people of the Iron Age had their own style of art and their own stories.

Speaking Celt-style

By the late Iron Age (roughly around 2,000 years ago) tribes with similar art and beliefs lived across the whole of northern Europe. We call them the Celts. They spoke languages that we would not recognise today, though a few of their words have survived in modern Welsh, Cornish and Gaelic.

Look!

A famous Celtic tale tells how a giant called Finn McCool built the rocks called the Giant's Causeway in Northern Ireland (above). He then used them as stepping stones to cross the sea to Scotland, to fight his enemies.

Swirls and circles

Celtic art is a type of decoration made from swirls and circles. It is usually found engraved on weapons and shields, such as the Battersea Shield (right). It was found in the River Thames in London, where it was probably thrown at some time between 350–50 BCE as an offering to Celtic gods and goddesses. Its beautiful swirly decorations are studded with 27 red enamel jewels.

Stories and music

The Celts never wrote things down but they passed stories on by word of mouth. Their myths and legends were like fairy tales full of magic and monsters. Some of our oldest British legends, especially Welsh and Irish myths, come from Celtic times. Tribes had their own poets, called bards, who told stories to everyone along with some accompanying harp or flute music.

If you lived in the Iron Age...

You might recognise some of these Celtic words, which have survived into modern times:

Abona – river (the origin of the name of the River Avon);

Dubris – waters (the origin of the name Dover);

Cantus – border (the origin of the name Kent);

Brocc – badger;

Torr – peak or high rock.

19

Buy and sell

Iron Age British tribes began to trade more and more with people in northern Europe. But what did they buy and sell?

On sale

Iron Age Britain became known across Europe for its wool, metals and wheat, but especially for its fine hunting dogs and slaves. Evidence of the slave trade was found in a lake in North Wales, where a heavy 5-m-long Iron Age slave chain was discovered.

If you lived in the Iron Age...

If your tribe fought with an enemy tribe and lost, you and all your family might be forced into slavery.

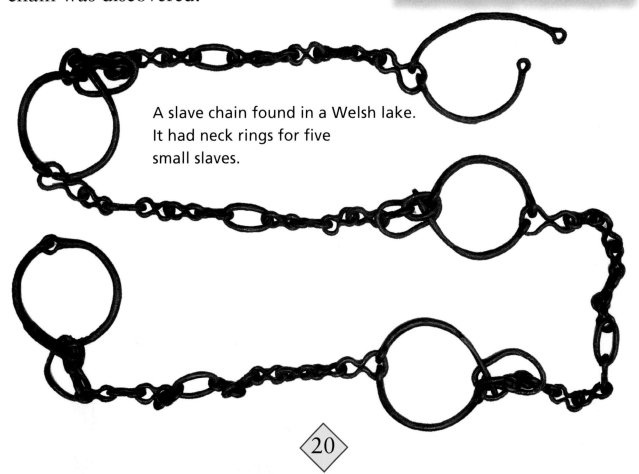

A slave chain found in a Welsh lake. It had neck rings for five small slaves.

British hunting dogs looked like Irish wolfhounds. They were highly prized. ▶

The Llyn Cerrig Bach slave chain has five neck rings to secure a line of slaves. The rings are very small, perhaps even for children. The chain was once thrown into the water, perhaps as an offering to Iron Age gods and goddesses.

Buying in

In the late Iron Age the wealthiest tribal leaders began to buy more and more luxury goods from abroad. They could afford olive oil, wine, glass and fine pottery brought in by wooden boats from abroad. Much of it was brought to a busy Iron Age port at Hengistbury Head in Dorset. Small hollowed-out log boats probably took the goods further inland along local rivers.

Hengistbury Head in Dorset, once a busy Iron Age port. ▼

Bury some treasure

In the late Iron Age British tribal leaders were getting very wealthy and powerful. They were rather like local kings and queens.

A treasure hoard

We sometimes call the wealthiest most powerful people in the land the 'elite'. In the late Iron Age the elite were far wealthier than everyone else in the country. An example of this is the breathtaking pile of golden Iron Age treasure found at Snettisham in Norfolk. It was buried around 75 BCE, and probably belonged to a local tribal leader. It might have been buried for safekeeping or perhaps to please Celtic gods.

◀ The Snettisham Hoard was found by a ploughman in Norfolk.

Look!

When gold comes out of the ground, even after many centuries, it still looks new and shiny. The ploughman who found the first pieces of the Snettisham Hoard thought he had unearthed bits of a modern brass bedstead.

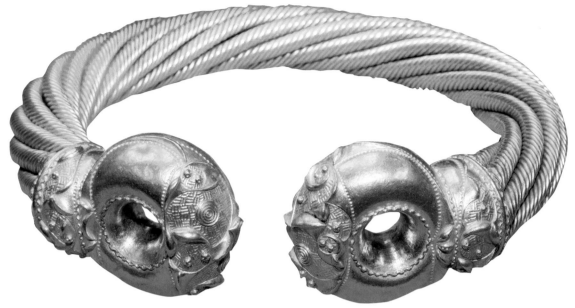

Top torcs

The Snettisham Hoard of gold and silver weighed around 35 kg in all. It included bracelets, ingots (bars of metal) and torcs – heavy neck rings made with twisted gold or silver wire. These were probably worn by leaders to show their power and wealth. There were an amazing 175 torcs in the hoard altogether. One of the finest gold ones is pictured above.

The chief's coins

In the late Iron Age, tribal leaders began to have their own coins made, with their personal symbols on (you can see an Iron Age coin on p7). There

▲ A gold torc, perhaps once worn by an Iron Age tribal leader.

were some of these coins in the Snettisham Hoard. A chief's symbol on a coin would have sent a message to anyone who saw it: "*I am so important that I even have my own coins!*".

If you lived in the Iron Age...

In the late Iron Age you would have lived in a busier place than your ancestors (see p4). There were probably around two million people living in Britain by then.

Find some mysteries

In the late Iron Age people in other parts of Europe wrote about the Britons, mentioning British religious leaders called Druids, who were very important and powerful.

I know what will happen

The Druids never wrote anything down about themselves, so we only know about them from other people's writing. It seems that they were very powerful, and chieftains listened to their advice about whether to fight battles or not. People may have believed that the Druids could predict what would happen in the future.

Predicting spoons

Divination spoons may once have been used by Druids to predict (divine) the future. They are usually found in pairs, one with a tiny hole and one marked into four quarters (this set was found in Penbryn in Wales).

Look!

It was said that the British Druids held religious ceremonies outdoors where they sacrificed animals and even humans. We can't know whether this was true, though.

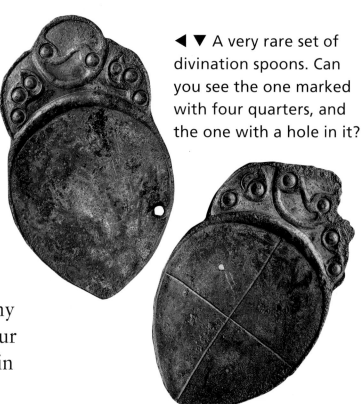

◄ ▼ A very rare set of divination spoons. Can you see the one marked with four quarters, and the one with a hole in it?

The divination spoons might have been clamped together so that liquid could be blown in through the hole. The Druids may have believed that the pattern the liquid made on the spoon inside could be used to predict the future.

Is this a Druid?

The Iron Age man shown on the right was buried around 2,200 years ago at Deal in Kent. He had a sword and shield but he was also wearing a finely made circle of bronze around his head. We know that in slightly later times this was the kind of headgear worn by religious leaders in Britain, so perhaps this man was a Druid as well as a warrior.

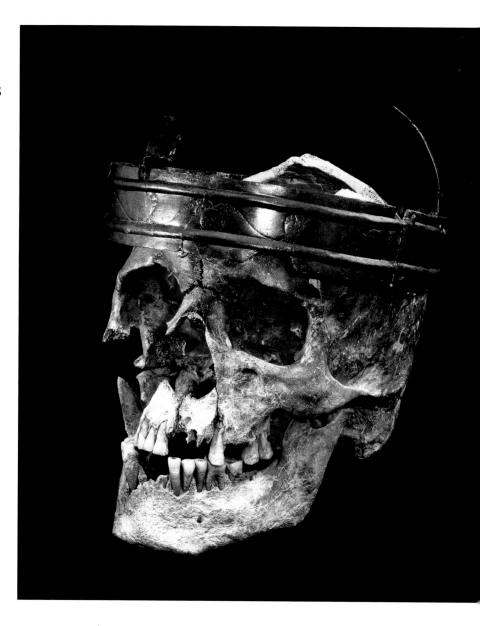

The headgear on this man's skull might mean he was a Druid, but nobody knows for sure. ▶

The Romans arrive

In 55 BCE the Roman army arrived in Britain, led by Julius Caesar. He landed his men on a beach near Dover, and Iron Age warriors were waiting on the shore to fight them.

This illustration shows how Roman legionaries (troops) may have looked when they first arrived in Britain in 55 BCE. ▼

If you lived in the Iron Age...

In the late Iron Age you would probably have heard of Rome, and if you lived in the far south you might even have seen some of Caesar's Roman soldiers when they first visited.

New friends and enemies

Julius Caesar's forces had to fight local tribes, but it soon became clear that the Romans were stronger. Some southern British chieftains quickly offered to help them. Caesar left with his army a year or so later, probably leaving friendly chieftains in control on his behalf and taking some of their sons back to Rome to be educated in Roman ways.

An Iron Age town

Southern Iron Age Britain began to copy Roman ways. For instance, around 50 BCE the Iron Age Atrebates (*at-reb-ar-tees*) tribe founded a Roman-inspired town we now call Silchester in Hampshire. For the first time that we know of in Britain, the town was planned out and the houses were built along a grid of gravel roads.

Eating Roman-style

The Iron Age people living in Silchester began to flavour their food with new-style Roman

Look!

The Atrebates living in Silchester may have liked trendy Roman food but they still had ancient Iron Age traditions. They ceremonially sacrificed and buried animals such as ravens and dogs around the town.

plants and herbs such as onions, celery, coriander and fennel. They brought Roman wine and olive oil in big jars called amphorae. We know they ate olives because the earliest olive stone ever found in Britain was discovered in Silchester, dating to the late Iron Age.

▼ Iron Age Britons began to use Roman wine and olive oil, kept in pottery jars like this.

See a last stand

By 43 CE some British Iron Age tribes were causing trouble for the Romans, attacking the chieftains that were friendly to Rome. This led to a Roman army landing in Britain once again, this time to stay.

Here come the Romans

Some tribes tried to fight back, but the Roman army was much better trained and armed. Soon the whole of the south-east was under direct Roman control and Roman troops began pressing onwards. We know that some tribes made last stands, but they could not match the powerful ballistas (mechanised crossbows) of the Romans.

Look!

This time the Roman troops stayed, and the period we call the Iron Age was at an end. The Romans gradually took control of England and Wales, though they never tried to conquer Scotland or Ireland.

Roman re-enactors load a ballista (a powerful crossbow). ▼

Battles on the hills

At Hod Hill hill fort in Dorset archaeologists found the ground peppered with Roman ballista bolts, while piles of stones gathered by the defenders, ready to throw or fire in slings, were left unused. That probably means the fort surrendered quickly to the attacking Romans. Meanwhile at Maiden Castle in Dorset (see p6) a skeleton was found with a Roman ballista bolt still lodged in its spine (see above).

Destroying the Druids

Roman writings tell of the Druid stronghold on the Isle of Anglesey being destroyed by

▲ A Roman ballista bolt was found in this skeleton from Maiden Castle.

Roman troops, who smashed the altars there and killed the priests and priestesses who fought against them. The Druids opposed the Romans and had probably persuaded some British tribes to try to drive them out.

If you lived in the Iron Age...

Under the new Roman rule ordinary British people would probably have lived in much the same way as before. But Celtic chieftains and Druid priests no longer ruled the land.

Glossary

Afterlife The idea of a new life lived by people after they have died on Earth. Iron Age people probably believed in an afterlife.

Amphorae Pottery jars used by the Romans to store olive oil or wine.

Ballista A mechanical crossbow used by the Roman army.

Bard Someone who told stories and played music in an Iron Age tribe.

Broch An Iron Age stone tower in northern Scotland.

Celts Tribes who lived across northern Europe roughly 2,000 years ago, who shared beliefs and ways of living.

Crannog An Iron Age roundhouse built on a platform over a lake.

Divination Predicting the future.

Druid A religious leader in Iron Age Britain.

Firedog A part of a meat spit used for roasting meat over a fire.

Foraging Gathering food in the wild.

Furnace A container used for heating metal to a high temperature, to soften it.

Hill fort A settlement built on top of a hill, surrounded by defences such as earth banks and ditches.

Hoard Hidden treasure.

Iron Age The period of time in Britain between 800 BCE and 43 CE (roughly between 2,000 and 3,000 years ago).

Iron ore Rocks containing iron.

Palisade Wooden stakes lined up to make a high fence.

Peat Plants that have rotted down to make soil, over many centuries. Chemicals in peat help to preserve ancient buried objects.

Pretani An ancient name for the British, meaning 'painted people'.

Quern A stone used to grind grain by hand to make flour.

Roundhouse A round hut with a thatched roof.

Sickle A curved sharp blade for cutting down crops.

Further information

Weblinks

http://www.theroundhouse.org/index.htm
Find out where to visit a reconstructed Iron Age roundhouse near you.

http://www.museumwales.ac.uk/2338/
See the finest Iron Age treasures found in Wales.

http://www.britishmuseum.org/explore/online_tours/britain/the_wetwang_chariot_burial/the_wetwang_chariot_burial.aspx
Find out all about the burial of an important woman in the Iron Age, and see a reconstruction of her chariot.

http://www.britishmuseum.org/explore/young_explorers1.aspx
All sorts of activities for young history explorers.

Note to parents and teachers: Every effort has been made by the Publishers to ensure that the web sites in this book are suitable for children, that they are of the highest educational value, and that they contain no inappropriate or offensive material. However, because of the nature of the Internet, it is impossible to guarantee that the contents of these sites will not be altered. We strongly advise that Internet access is supervised by a responsible adult.

Timeline

800–700 BCE The first hill forts were built in Britain.

700–500 BCE Iron-making became more widespread.

500–100 BCE Big hill forts were built, such as Maiden Castle in Dorset.

500–200 BCE The first brochs (stone towers) were built in northern Scotland.

330 BCE An ancient Greek explorer called Pytheas sailed round Britain and became the first person to write about it.

100 BCE British coins were made for the first time.

55 BCE The Roman army arrived, led by Julius Caesar. The Roman forces left around a year later.

52 BCE An Iron Age town was founded in what we now call Silchester in Hampshire. Other Iron Age towns followed.

43 BCE The Romans returned to conquer and rule southern Britain.

Index